REVISED AND UPDATED

AMAZING JOURNEYS

Across the Solar System

Rod Theodorou

Heinemann Library
Chicago, Illinois

Designed by Victoria Bevan, Michelle Lisseter, and Bridge Creative Services
Illustrations by Stephen Lings and Jane Pickering at Linden Artists
Printed and bound in China by WKT

10 09 08 07 06
10 9 8 7 6 5 4 3 2 1

New edition ISBN: 1 4034 8788 X (hardback)
                   1 4034 8795 2 (paperback)

The Library of Congress cataloged the first edition as follows:
Theodorou, Rod
    Across the solar system / Rod Theodorou.
       p. cm. -- (Amazing journeys)
    Includes bibliographical references and index.
    Summary: Takes the reader on a journey through the solar system, describing comets, asteroids, and
the planets, including their average temperature, length of day, distance from the sun, and more.
    ISBN 1-57572-486-3 (lib. bdg.)
    1. Solar system -- Juvenile literature. [1. Solar system. 2. Planets.]
I. Title. II. Series: Theodorou, Rod. Amazing journeys.
QB501.3.T48 2000
523.2--dc21
    99-37162
    CIP

Acknowledgements
The publishers would like to thank the following for permission to reproduce photographs:
Corbis/epa/NASA p. **27**; Oxford Scientific Films: NASA pp. **16**, **17**; Science Photo Library: European
Space Agency p. **10**; Ludek Pesek p. **23**; Mehau Kulyk p. **11**; NASA pp. **13**, **14**, **15**, **17**, **19**, **20**, **21**, **22**,
24, **25**, **26**; National Optical Astronomy Observatories p. **11**; US Geological Survey pp. **12**, **18**; Victor
Habbick Visions p. **6**.

Cover artwork of the solar system reproduced with permission of Science Photo Library/ Detlev
van Ravenswaay.

The publishers would like to thank Nick Sample for his assistance in the preparation of this book.

Every effort has been made to contact copyright holders of any material reproduced in this book.
Any omissions will be rectified in subsequent printings if notice is given to the publishers.

The paper used to print this book comes from sustainable resources.

Disclaimer
All the Internet addresses (URLs) given in this book were valid at the time of going to press. However,
due to the dynamic nature of the Internet, some addresses may have changed, or sites may have
changed or ceased to exist since publication. While the author and publishers regret any inconvenience
this may cause readers, no responsibility for any such changes can be accepted by either the author or
the publishers.

Contents

Some words are shown in bold, **like this.** You can find out what these words mean by looking in the Glossary.

Introduction

You are about to go on an amazing journey. You are going to climb inside a spaceship that is more advanced than anything that exists today. You are going to travel to the center of our **solar system**, across millions of miles, to witness our blazing, spectacular Sun. Then, you are going to travel away from the Sun, across silent, cold, black space. You are going to visit each of our solar system's nine planets, from the dead, colorless world of Mercury to the dazzling, rainbow storm clouds of Jupiter.

As you visit the planets, you will learn how different they are and how precious our own planet is. Earth is the only planet in the solar system that can support millions of life forms.

1	Sun
2	Mercury
3	Venus
4	Earth
5	Mars
6	Jupiter
7	Saturn
8	Uranus
9	Neptune
10	Pluto

The first four "inner" planets are small, rocky worlds. Four of the "outer" planets are "gas giants"—huge balls of gases and liquids. Pluto is the smallest and farthest planet from the Sun.

Outer planets

Inner planets

All the planets in our solar system move around the Sun (*solar* means "of the Sun"). The Sun is a huge ball of exploding gases called a **star**. There are billions of other stars in our **galaxy**. Many of them also have planets **orbiting** in their own solar systems.

Our spaceship is designed to travel at incredible speed. Its **hull** can withstand crushing **pressures** as well as intense heat and cold. We are going to need it, because we are going to explore places that nobody has ever set foot on before. What will they be like? Could they support other forms of life?

The spaceship's engines fire up. You are about to find out.

1	*Sun*
2	*Mercury*
3	*Venus*
4	*Earth*
5	*Mars*
6	*Jupiter*
7	*Saturn*
8	*Uranus*
9	*Neptune*
10	*Pluto*

The planets move around the Sun in an **oval** path called an orbit. Earth orbits the Sun just like any other planet. An Earth year is the time it takes to orbit the Sun once.

Journey Map

Here is a map of our space journey. We head straight for the Sun and go as near as we can before turning and heading out toward the planets. On our way, we will see many huge lumps of rock and metal tumbling through space. These **asteroids orbit** the Sun just like the planets. We may also see **comets**. Comets are like huge, dirty icebergs shooting through space. As they break up and melt, they leave a "tail" of gas and dust behind them that is millions of miles long. As we visit some planets, we will also see their moons. Moons are huge balls of rock and ice that orbit around some planets.

Mars

Earth

Mercury

Page 18

Page 10

Venus

Page 12

Page 16

Page 14

Comet

Sun

Pluto

Saturn

Neptune

Page 26

Moons

Page 25

Uranus

Page 24

Page 22

Jupiter

Page 20

Asteroids

DATABANK EXPLAINED

The spaceship's databank gives you important information about each planet we visit.

Diameter tells you how wide the planet is.

Earth

Diameter
7,927 miles
(12,756 km)

Length of day is how long it takes from sunrise to sunrise, measured in Earth time.

Length of year is how long the planet takes to orbit the Sun, measured in Earth time.

The Blazing Sun

Our spaceship crosses 93 million miles (150 million kilometers) in just a few minutes. Temperature **gauges** go higher and higher as we approach the center of our **solar system**: the Sun. It is huge—one million times bigger than Earth! It fills our **protective** screens until all we can see is red fire.

The Sun is like an enormous **nuclear** explosion. Its surface is a bubbling, boiling mass of burning gases. It has been burning for five billion years. In another six billion years, it will grow in size to become an even bigger flaming ball, called a red giant. When this happens, Earth and all life in our solar system will be destroyed.

Without the Sun's warmth, there would be no life on Earth. Plants use the Sun's **energy** to grow. Without plants, animals would have nothing to feed on.

DATABANK

Distance from Earth	93 million miles (150 million kilometers)
Diameter	865,318 miles (1,392,530 kilometers)
Size comparison	

Earth Sun

Average temperature	Surface: 10,000 °F (5,500 °C)
	Inside: 27 million °F (15 million °C)
Number of planets	9

WARNING!

This spaceship is fitted with protective screens. Looking directly at the Sun is dangerous. Never look at the Sun through **binoculars** or a **telescope**. It can blind you!

Solar flares

Sometimes huge jets of flame **erupt** from the Sun's surface and shoot out into space.

Sunspots

The Sun appears to have black areas on its surface. These "sunspots" are places where the surface is slightly cooler. Sunspots can be as big as Earth.

Mercury: The Dead World

Touchdown! We have landed on the first of the four "inner" planets. Tiny Mercury is only one-twentieth the size of Earth. It is the nearest planet to the Sun. It has almost no blanket of **atmosphere** around it to protect it from the Sun's rays or to keep the warmth in at night. There is never any gust of wind or any drop of rain. There are no clouds and no colors in the sky. Even though it is daytime, we can see twinkling stars and the huge Sun, which looks three times bigger than it does from Earth.

A day lasts two Earth months here. As we land, we can feel the intense heat and **radiation**. We are glad our spaceship's **hull** can withstand the heat, which is four times hotter than boiling water. That is hot enough to melt lead! When the night does come, temperatures will drop far below the freezing point.

Mercury is only slightly bigger than our own Moon. This photo, taken by the Mariner 10 **space probe**, shows that it also looks like our Moon.

DATABANK

Distance from the Sun 36 million miles (58 million kilometers)

Diameter 3,032 miles (4,879 kilometers)

Size comparison

Earth   Mercury

Average temperature
Day: 720 °F (400 °C)
Night: -300 °F (-170 °C)

Length of day 58·5 Earth days

Length of year 88 Earth days

Number of moons 0

Craters

A crater is the round "scar" left by a **meteorite** smashing into a planet, just like a pebble thrown into sand. Mercury's landscape is blasted with huge craters made by meteorites that showered the planet millions of years ago.

Caloris Basin

These small craters are inside the largest crater in the **solar system**. It was caused by an enormous **asteroid** hitting Mercury, throwing out crater walls the size of mountains.

Venus: Our Savage Sister

Venus is often called our **twin** or sister planet. Named after the ancient Roman goddess of beauty, it is the closest planet to Earth and is almost the same size. It is also the brightest planet visible from Earth. However, there is one thing that makes Venus a very different sister: its **atmosphere**.

Venus has a cloudy atmosphere so thick it presses down on the surface like a million blankets. If we stepped outside our spaceship, we would be crushed as flat as paper. No heat can escape from the atmosphere. It is like being trapped inside a huge greenhouse, with temperatures rising even higher than on Mercury. This "greenhouse effect" causes **sulfuric acid** to rain down from the violent storms above.

We do not stay long on Venus.

This picture of the surface of Venus is made up of many smaller photographs taken by the Magellan space probe. It spent four years in **orbit** around Venus.

DATABANK

Distance from the Sun	67 million miles (108 million kilometers)
Diameter	7,521 miles (12,104 kilometers)
Size comparison	

Earth   Venus

Average temperature	900 °F (480 °C)
Length of day	243 Earth days
Length of year	224.5 Earth days
Number of moons	0

Visitors to Venus

Four Russian *Venera* **space probes** have landed on Venus and photographed its surface. It is hot, dry, and quite smooth. Storms and high **pressure** have **eroded** many of the mountains and hills.

Magellan Probe

In 1989 the *Magellan* probe was launched, and in 1990 it sent back photos of Venus. They showed that there may once have been oceans on Venus, but these boiled away millions of years ago.

Earth: The Water Planet

Our spaceship takes us into an **orbit** around our own planet. As we circle over the Pacific Ocean, all we can see is blue water. After the violent acid storms of Venus, Earth looks gentle and welcoming.

Earth's **atmosphere** protects its surface like a blanket from the intense heat of the Sun on one side and from the coldness of space on the other. If it were much colder, all the water would turn to ice. If it were much hotter, all the water would boil away. Earth is the only planet where the temperature is just right for lots of liquid water. The atmosphere also keeps in plenty of air. It is the warmth of the Sun, the water, and the air that make Earth just the right kind of planet for living things to survive.

White storm clouds swirl above Earth's surface.

DATABANK

Distance from the Sun	93 million miles (150 million kilometers)
Diameter	7,927 miles (12,756 kilometers)
Size comparison	

Earth   Moon

Average temperature	57 °F (14 °C)
Length of day	24 hours
Length of year	365.25 days
Number of moons	1

The Moon

The Moon is a dead world, much like Mercury. It has no atmosphere, and so it has no air, no blue sky, no water, and no weather. It orbits Earth once every 27.3 days. Twelve people have landed on its surface.

Seas without water

The Moon's surface is heavily cratered from **meteorites** and **asteroids** crashing into its surface. Some of these asteroid collisions were so violent they melted the Moon's surface, flooding it with **lava**. These lava flows left huge dark, flat patches that we call "seas."

Mars: The Red Planet

Our spaceship breaks out of Earth's **orbit** and crosses millions of miles to approach a planet about half the size of Earth. We land on its surface and soon see why Mars is called the red planet. This cold and dusty planet is covered in red dust. Sometimes the wind whips this up into huge, red sandstorms. In many ways, this is the most similar planet to Earth. It has a thin **atmosphere**, and a day lasts almost exactly the same time as on Earth. Out of our **portholes** we see a world quite similar to an Earth desert. The sky is pink, with a few wispy clouds. The wind blows across orange sand dunes, craters, huge dead **volcanoes**, and mountains. One of these, Olympus Mons, is the largest volcano in the **solar system**. It is three times higher than Mount Everest!

This shows the surface of Mars, as photographed by the *Viking Orbiter*.

DATABANK

Distance from the Sun	142 million miles (228 million kilometers)
Diameter	4,222 miles (6,794 kilometers)
Size comparison	

Earth   Mars

Average temperature	-81 °F (-63 °C)
Length of day	24 Earth hours
Length of year	687 Earth days
Number of moons	2

Waterworld

Many scientists believe that millions of years ago, Mars was a warmer planet and had its own seas. Now, the water is gone, but we can still see what look like dried-up riverbeds. This photo was taken by the *Viking Orbiter*.

Martians?

In 1984 a **meteorite** that appears to be a lump of rock from Mars landed on Earth. Some scientists think it has tiny **fossils** of **bacteria** on its surface. Could this mean there was once life on Mars?

Jupiter: Gas Giant

As we get nearer and nearer to Jupiter, we can hardly believe its size. It is the largest planet in the **solar system**—1,266 times bigger than Earth. Its surface is beautiful. It looks like white, red, brown, and orange paints, swirling and mixing. A giant red eye on its surface seems to look at us. Our spaceship plunges straight into its churning **atmosphere**. We travel down through thick, white, and orange clouds that flash with lightning, then into bluish, icy water droplets, and finally into gases so thick it is almost like being underwater. It gets darker and darker. Somewhere beneath us is the rocky **core**. The incredible heat and **pressure** outside are damaging our **hull**. We turn around and head for space.

Jupiter is a giant ball of gases.

Distance from the Sun	483 million miles (778 million kilometers)
Diameter	88,850 miles (142,984 kilometers)
Size comparison	

Earth

Jupiter

Average temperature	-238 °F (-150 °C)
Length of day	10 Earth hours
Length of year	12 Earth years
Number of moons	16

The red spot

Jupiter is a planet of incredible storms. The Great Red Spot is the largest storm in the solar system. This massive **hurricane**, three times wider than Earth, has been raging for 300 years!

Life on Europa?

Europa is one of Jupiter's many moons. Scientists think there may be a 62-mile (100-kilometer) deep ocean beneath its icy surface. If this ocean also contains underwater **volcanoes**, the water and heat needed to support life may exist.

Saturn: The Ringed Planet

We are now into deep space, many millions of miles from Earth. A huge and amazing planet fills our viewing screens. Saturn is the second largest of the planets. It is very similar to Jupiter and just as beautiful. Like Jupiter, it is a huge ball of gases with an inner **core** of rock and ice. Around the planet are huge, flat rings made from lumps of rock and ice that **orbit** the planet like billions of tiny moons.

We do not enter Saturn's **atmosphere**. Like Jupiter, it is a planet of amazing storms. Winds can blow up to 1,120 miles (1,800 kilometers) per hour! Beneath the stormy surface are hundreds of miles of thick, heavy gases, ice, and water **vapor**.

Saturn is covered in hazy yellow clouds.

DATABANK

Distance from the Sun	888 million miles (1,429 million kilometers)
Diameter	74,901 miles (120,536 kilometers)
Size comparison	

Earth   Saturn

Average temperature	-292 °F (-180 °C)
Length of day	10.5 Earth hours
Length of year	29.5 Earth years
Number of moons	18

Saturn's rings

We do not know exactly how Saturn's rings were made. Some scientists think Saturn pulled lots of space "rubble" into its orbit millions of years ago. Others think a giant **asteroid** may have hit and destroyed a small moon, leaving rings of rubble and ice. Most think they may have been formed like this:

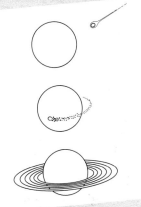

1. A giant asteroid got caught in Saturn's orbit.

2. As it was pulled around the planet, it started to break up.

3. The rings are the remains of the asteroid and still orbit the planet.

23

Uranus: The Green Planet

Uranus is the third largest planet. As we approach it, we can see its eleven rings, but they are not as beautiful as the bright, icy rings of Saturn. They are very thin and hard to see because they are made from black lumps of rock and fine black dust. Thick, green-blue gases cover the planet in a cloudy fog. What lies beneath this smoggy layer? Only one **space probe**, *Voyager 2*, has ever flown past this gas giant. We think it is made from thick gases surrounding a rocky **core**. We dare not risk damage to our spaceship, so we continue our journey.

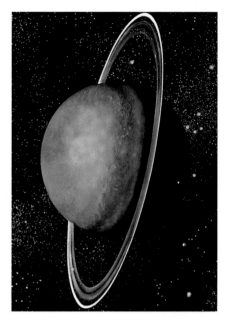

This is an artist's painting of Uranus, showing the thin rings.

DATABANK

Distance from the Sun	1,784 million miles (2,871 million kilometers)
Diameter	31,770 miles (51,118 kilometers)
Size comparison	

Earth   Uranus

Average temperature	-353 °F (-214 °C)
Length of day	17 Earth hours
Length of year	84 Earth years
Number of moons	15

Neptune: The Blue Planet

This blue-green planet is similar to Uranus. It is a gas giant, and it also has thin, dark rings of dust and rock. We are careful not to get too close to Neptune's surface. This is a freezing-cold world with violent storms as big as Earth! Winds here can travel at incredible speeds, up to 1,240 miles (2,000 kilometers) per hour—the fastest in the **solar system**. We see a streak of wispy clouds known as the "scooter," which travels completely around the giant planet every sixteen hours!

It is easy to see why Neptune was named after the Roman god of the sea.

DATABANK

Distance from the Sun	2,798 million miles (4,504 million kilometers)
Diameter	30,777 miles (49,528 kilometers)
Size comparison	

Earth

Neptune

Average temperature	-364 °F (-220 °C)
Length of day	19 Earth hours
Length of year	165 Earth years
Number of moons	8

Pluto: Mystery Planet

Far away in the distance, we can see Pluto, the planet farthest from the Sun in the **solar system**. It is a tiny planet, smaller than our own Moon. It is so far away, even the most powerful **telescopes** cannot discover much about its surface. We know it must be a very cold planet, covered in layers of ice and frozen gases. Some scientists think Pluto may not even be a true planet. It may simply be a large **comet**. Warning signs flash in our spaceship. Unless we turn around now, we will not have enough fuel to get back to Earth. Pluto will have to remain a mystery. It is time to go home.

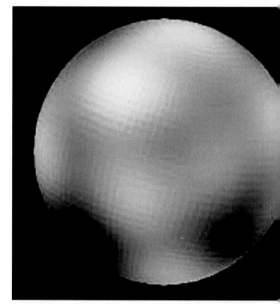

Pluto is too far away for us to photograph in any detail.

DATABANK

Distance from the Sun	3,675 million miles (5,914 million kilometers)
Diameter	1,442 miles (2,320 kilometers)
Size comparison	Earth Pluto
Average temperature	-382 °F (-230 °C)
Length of day	6.5 Earth days
Length of year	249 Earth years
Number of moons	3

Exploring Space: Planet Probe

Of course, the spaceship we used in this book does not yet exist. All the information comes from what we have discovered from telescopes and **space probes**. Some of the probes sent into space simply **orbit** planets, sending pictures and other information back to Earth by radio signals. Others are built to enter a planet's **atmosphere** and even land on the surface. The picture on the right shows how one probe, *Sojourner*, visited Mars in 1997. The planets are so far away it would take a lot of money and time to build a spaceship that could visit even Mars, the closest of them. For the moment, scientists are building space stations to orbit Earth. These tell us more about how to live in space. Perhaps it is only a matter of time before humans can make amazing journeys across the solar system.

The Mars Exploration Rover set off for Mars in 2003.

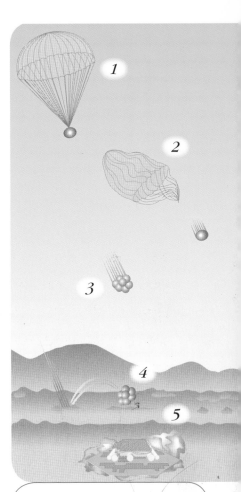

1 *The* Mars Pathfinder *pod parachutes down to the surface of Mars.*
2 *The parachutes are released.*
3 *Large balloons inflate around the pod.*
4 *The pod bounces down on the surface.*
5 *The pod opens to release* Sojourner.

Glossary

asteroid	small planet, less than 310 miles (500 kilometers) wide, found in a belt between Mars and Jupiter in our solar system
atmosphere	mixture of gases around Earth, a star, or a planet
bacteria	tiny organisms that live in the soil, in water, and in the bodies of animals and plants; they can be helpful or harmful
binoculars	instrument with lenses for both eyes, used to make faraway objects look nearer and clearer
comet	object in space made from gas, dust, and ice that travels around the Sun in an orbit
core	center of something
cosmonaut	Russian astronaut
energy	having the ability to work or be active
erode	to wear away
erupt	to explode or shoot out material such as lava and rock
fossil	remains of a living thing, saved in or turned into rock
galaxy	one of the millions of enormous collections of stars, other solar systems, dust, and gases that make up space
gauge	instrument for measuring or testing something
hull	frame of a ship
hurricane	very strong wind of at least 75 miles (120 kilometers) per hour
lava	hot, melting rock that comes out of an erupting volcano or cracks in a planet or moon's surface

meteorite	small, solid object that falls from space and hits a planet with incredible impact
nuclear	something related to or powered by nuclear energy
orbit	path of a planet or satellite around another object in space
oval	shaped like a circle stretched one way
porthole	window in the side of a ship
pressure	weight of something pressing or being pressed
protective	something that is designed to take care of you or shield you
radiation	when energy is sent out in strong rays
satellite	something that moves around another, bigger object
solar system	the nine planets and the comets and asteroids that orbit around the Sun
space probe	spacecraft that sends information back to Earth about space
star	large object, such as the Sun, that is very hot and makes its own energy by nuclear reactions
sulfuric acid	thick, colorless, oily liquid that is a dangerous acid made from sulfur
telescope	instrument, with only one lens to look through, that makes distant objects seem nearer and larger
twin	one of a pair of identical or similar things
vapor	gas, like mist, that occurs when some substances are heated
volcano	hole or crack in Earth's crust through which lava, hot gases, rocks, and ash sometimes explode

Space Calendar

October 1957	The Soviet Union launches *Sputnik 1*, the first man-made **satellite** to **orbit** Earth.
April 1961	Yuri Gagarin becomes the first human to fly into space.
June 1963	**Cosmonaut** Valentina Tereshkova becomes the first woman in space.
July 1969	*Apollo 11* lands on the Moon. On July 21, Neil Armstrong is the first human to walk on the Moon.
May 1971	The Soviet **space probe** *Mars* 3 lands on Mars.
October 1975	The Soviet probe *Venera 9* lands on Venus.
April 1981	The first space shuttle, *Columbia*, is launched into space.
July 1997	NASA's *Pathfinder* visits Mars and *Sojourner* sends back photographs from the surface.
April 2001	The world's first space tourist takes a trip into space. Dennis Tito pays $20 million for his voyage to the International Space Station.
January 2004	Two buggies, *Spirit* and *Opportunity*, land on Mars.
March 2004	Astronomers discover a new planet-like **asteroid** orbiting the Sun. They nickname it Sedna.
July 2005	Astronomers discover another planet-like object. They nickname it Xena. Some scientists think it is an asteroid. But Xena is bigger than Pluto and orbits the Sun. Could this be the tenth planet?
January 2006	A spacecraft called *New Horizons* is launched on a mission to Pluto and beyond.

Find Out More

Further reading

Bond, Peter. *DK Guide to Space*. New York: Dorling Kindersley, 2004.

Goldsmith, Mike. *Solar System*. Boston: Kingfisher, 2004.

Oxlade, Chris. *The Mystery of Life on Other Planets*. Chicago: Heinemann Library, 2002.

Organization

National Aeronautics and Space Administration (NASA)

300 E. Street SW
Washington, D.C. 20546-0001

www.nasa.gov

Using the Internet

If you want to find out more about the solar system, you can go to one of these website addresses. Otherwise, you can use a search engine, such as www.yahooligans.com or www.internet4kids.com, and type in keywords such as "solar system" or a related subject such as "asteroids."

Websites

www.nasa.gov/audience/forkids/home/index.html

NASA has many Internet sites, including this one for kids.

www.space.com

This website is packed with the latest space news and photos.

www.seds.org/billa/tnp/

This "multimedia tour of the solar system" describes the history, mythology, and current scientific thinking about the planets, moons, and other objects in the solar system.

Index